P9-AGN-900

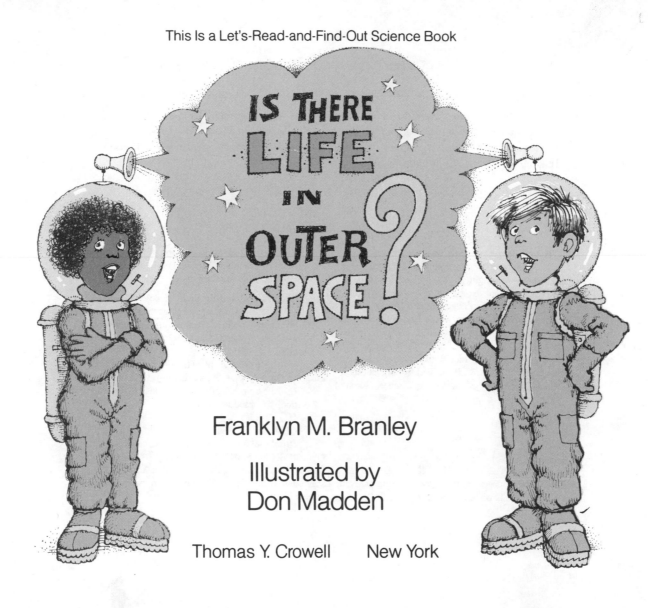

IS THERE LIFE IN OUTER SPACE?

Franklyn M. Branley

Illustrated by
Don Madden

Thomas Y. Crowell   New York

The *Let's-Read-and-Find-Out Science Book* series was originated by Dr. Franklyn M. Branley, Astronomer Emeritus and former Chairman of the American Museum–Hayden Planetarium, and was formerly co-edited by him and Dr. Roma Gans, Professor Emeritus of Childhood Education, Teachers College, Columbia University.

Is There Life in Outer Space?
Text copyright © 1984 by Franklyn M. Branley
Illustrations copyright © 1984 by Don Madden
All rights reserved. No part of this book may be used or reproduced in any manner whatsoever without written permission except in the case of brief quotations embodied in critical articles and reviews. Printed in the United States of America. For information address Thomas Y. Crowell Junior Books, 10 East 53rd Street, New York, N.Y. 10022. Published simultaneously in Canada by Fitzhenry & Whiteside Limited, Toronto,

3 4 5 6 7 8 9 10

Library of Congress Cataloging in Publication Data
Branley, Franklyn Mansfield, 1915-
    Is there life in outer space?

  (Let's-read-and-find-out science book)
    Summary: Discusses some of the ideas and misconceptions about life in outer space and speculates on the existence of such life in light of recent space explorations.
    1. Life on other planets—Juvenile literature.
2. Outer space—Exploration—Juvenile literature.
[1. Life on other planets. 2. Outer space—Exploration] I. Madden, Don, 1927- , ill. II. Title.
III. Series.
QB54.B694 1984   574.999   83-45057
ISBN 0-690-04374-0
ISBN 0-690-04375-9 (lib. bdg.)

Photo credits: pages 13, 14, 17, and 19 from the National Aeronautics and Space Administration; page 28, photographs of Yoda and Chewbacca from Lucasfilm Ltd., © Lucasfilm Ltd. (LFL) 1980. All rights reserved.

Bears and birds, insects and toads, trees, flowers, and people live on planet Earth.

Do they live anywhere else? Do plants and animals live on the moon? Do they live on Mars or Jupiter or any other planet? For a long time people have wondered about that. Maybe you have, too.

5

More than a hundred years ago a newspaper said plants and animals lived on the moon. An astronomer could see them through a big, new telescope.

There were trees on the moon, the newspaper said. Big melons grew on them. Animals that looked like small buffaloes grazed beneath the trees. Animals that looked like bears walked around on their hind legs.

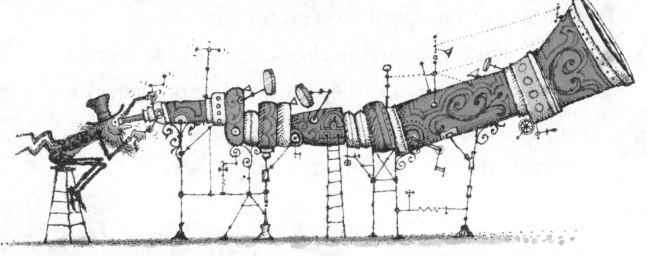

There were people, too. They had hair all over their bodies, and they had wings. The moon people were friendly, the story said. They sat near a pond feeding melons to one another.

The story wasn't true. But for a long time, people believed in these moon creatures.

People also believed a radio story that said Martians had landed on Earth. The Martians had big heads and small bodies. They came in spaceships. Once they landed, they spread out and attacked people in towns and villages.

By 1969, almost no one believed in moon creatures, or in Martians with big heads. Still, many people hoped that life would be found somewhere beyond Earth. In that year Neil Armstrong and Edwin Aldrin landed on the moon.

After them, other astronauts went to the moon. No matter where they looked, the astronauts found nothing alive. They found no sign that plants or animals have ever lived there. The moon is a dead world, and it always has been.

But, people said, that does not mean there is no other life in our solar system. Maybe there are plants on Mars. Maybe there are animals, too—although no one expected they would look like the Martians with big heads.

Photographs of Mars show wiggly lines on the planet. The lines look like riverbeds. Was there water on Mars? Where there is water, there may also be plants and animals. Did plants and animals once live on Mars? Could they be living there still?

Space probes were sent to Mars. More photographs were taken. The soil of Mars was tested. No plants or animals of any kind were seen in the photographs. No signs of life were found in the soil.

But what about the other planets? Perhaps there is life on Venus. Or maybe Mercury has plants and animals.

A probe was sent to Mercury to get a closer look. This is a picture that it took.

Mercury doesn't look like a place where plants or animals could live. It looks like the dead world of the moon. Also, Mercury gets very hot, much too hot for anything to live there.

Probes were landed on Venus, too. No signs of life were found. It is so hot on Venus that parts of some probes melted when they landed.

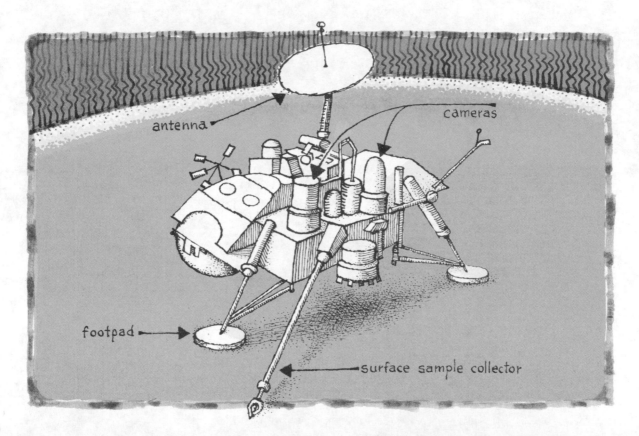

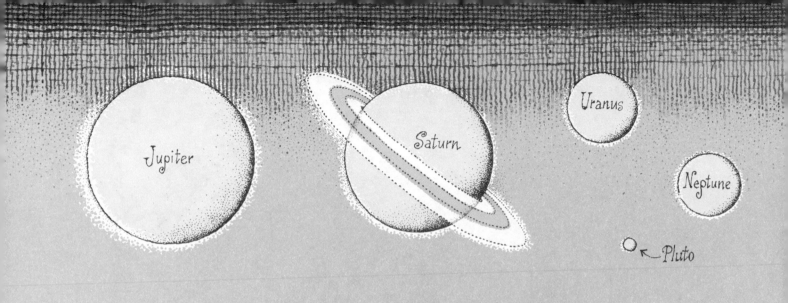

No one expects there could be life on any of the
other planets in our solar system.

Jupiter, Saturn, Uranus, and Neptune are covered
by poison gases. Also, those planets are very cold,
much colder than any place on Earth. And so is tiny
Pluto.

In our solar system, Earth seems to be the only planet where there is life.

But there may be other planets beyond our solar system, way out among the billions of stars.

There may be planets going around these stars, just as Earth goes around the sun.

If there are such planets, plants and animals may live on them.

If creatures do live in far-off worlds, they may look quite different from the plants and animals on Earth. They may have tiny bodies and big heads like the Martians.

They may have wings and hairy bodies like the
moon people.

28 Here's how the creators of the movie *The Empire Strikes Back* picture life in outer space.

They may have heavy legs with small arms and
hands. Perhaps they walk around on all fours. Or they
may look quite different from anything we can
imagine. Who knows?

Some people think it's silly to believe there are planets beyond our solar system. They say it's even sillier to believe there is life on them. But I don't think so.

It seems that somewhere out among the billions of stars, there must be plants and animals living on other worlds. There may be creatures that know as much as we do. Some may be a lot smarter.

One day we may be able to talk back and forth with them. Many years from now we may even travel to those far-off planets and land on them. That's what I think.

What do you think?